D0990299

4-14-75

COLLECTED POEMS

ORIGINALLY
PUBLISHED IN PARIS

The COLLECTED POEMS of Ernest Hemingway

PIRATED EDITION
SAN FRANCISCO
1960

HASKELL HOUSE PUBLISHERS LTD.
Publishers of Scarce Scholarly Books
NEW YORK, N. Y. 10012
1970

First Published 1960

HASKELL HOUSE PUBLISHERS LTD.
Publishers of Scarce Scholarly Books
280 LAFAYETTE STREET
NEW YORK, N. Y. 10012

Library of Congress Catalog Card Number: 79-100764

Standard Book Number 8383-0044-8

Printed in the United States of America

designed by Brayton

contents

MISCELLANEOUS POEMS

ULTIMATELY

He tried to spit out the truth;
Dry-mouthed at first,
He drooled and slobbered in the end;
Truth dribbling his chin.

THE LADY POET WITH FOOTNOTES

One lady poet was a nymphomaniac and wrote for Vanity Fair. (1)

One lady poet's husband was killed in the war. (2)

One lady poet wanted her lover but was afraid of having a baby. When she finally got married she found she couldn't have a baby. (3)

One lady poet slept with Bill Keely, got fatter and fatter and made half a million dollars writing bum plays. (4)

One lady poet had enough to eat. (5)

One lady poet was big and fat and no fool. (6)

---

(1) College nymph. Favorite lyric poet of leading editorial writer N. Y. Tribune.

(2) It sold her stuff.

(3) Favorite of State University male virgins. Wonderful on unrequited love.

(4) Stomach's gone bad from liquor. Expects to do something really good soon.

(5) It showed in her work.

(6) She smoked cigars all right, but her stuff was no good.

THE AGE DEMANDED

The age demanded that we sing
And cut away our tongue.

The age demanded that we flow
And hammered in the bung.

The age demanded that we dance
And jammed us into iron pants.

And in the end the age was handed
The sort of shit that it demanded.

THE ERNEST LIBERAL'S LAMENT

I know monks masturbate at night
That pet cats screw
That some girls bite
And yet
What can I do
To set things right?

THE SOUL OF SPAIN

[*In the manner of Gertrude Stein*]

In the rain in the rain in the rain in the rain in Spain.
Does it rain in Spain?
Oh yes my dear on the contrary and there are no bullfights.
The dancers dance in long white pants
It isn't right to yence your aunts
Come Uncle let us go home.
Home is where the heart is, home is where the fart is.
Come let us fart in the home.
There is no art in a fart.
Still a fart may not be artless.
Let us fart an artless fart in the home.

Democracy.
Democracy.
Bill says democracy must go.
Go democracy.
Go
Go
Go
Bill's father never knowingly would sit down at table
with a Democrat.

Now Bill says democracy must go.
Go on democracy.
Democracy is the shit.
Relativity is the shit.
Dictators are the shit.
Mencken is the shit.
Waldo Frank is the shit.
The Broom is the shit.
Dempsey is the shit.

They say Ezra is the shit.
But Ezra is nice.
Come let us build a monument to Ezra.
Good a very nice monument.
You did that nicely
Can you do another?
Let me try and do one.
Let us all try and do one.
Let the little girl over there on the corner try and do one.
Come on little girl.
Do one for Ezra.
Good.
You have all been successful children.
Now let us clean the mess up.
The Dial does a monument to Proust.
We have done a monument to Ezra.
A monument is a monument.
After all it is the spirit of the thing that counts.

PART TWO of THE SOUL OF SPAIN

You come to Spain but do not remain. Ann Veronica, Marcial Veronica, Pablo Veronica, Gitanillo Veronica. No they cannot veronica because the wind blows. The wind blows and it does not snows look at the bull with his bloody nose.

PART III

There is no night life in Spain. They stay up late but they get up late. That is not night life. That is delaying the day. Night life is when everybody says what the hell and you do not remember who paid the bill. Night life goes round and round and you look at the wall to make it stop. Night life comes out of a bottle and goes into a jar. If you think how much are the drinks it is not night life.

PART IV of the same story

After a while there were no bullfights. What the hell no bullfights? No bullfights. No you really can't mean it no bull-fights. But there were no bullfights.

PART V follows

We got on a train and went somewhere else.

PART V

A serious and vivid account of a divertissement in the cruel sport.

Estocada stuck well stuck. They run round in circles with the capes and the bull whirls round and round and then goes down and folds his knees under and his tongue sticks out and the sword sticks out dully the hilt and the bandillas stick out sharply at angles. Well stuck by the applauded diestro. Well stuck by the afamoused espada. They are going to kill him back of the horns with the short knife.

Short knives are thick short knives are quickshort knives make a needed nick.

I love to see the puntillo used. It is exactly like turning off an electric light bulb.

*NEO-THOMIST POEM

The Lord is my shepherd, I shall not
want him for long.

*"The title 'Neo-Thomist Poem' refers to temporary embracing of church by literary gents — E. H."

TEN POEMS

from

Three Stories and Ten Poems,

Paris, 1923.

MITRAIGLIATRICE

The mills of the gods grind slowly
But the mill
Chatters in mechanical staccato.
Ugly short infantry of the mind,
Advancing over difficult terrain.
Making this Corona
Their mitrailleuse.

OKLAHOMA

All of the Indians are dead
(a good Indian is a dead Indian)
Or riding in motor cars —
(the oil lands, you know, they're all rich)
Smoke smarts my eyes,
Cottonwood twigs and buffalo dung
Smoke grey in the tepee —
(or is it my myopic trachoma)

The prairies are long,
The moon rises
Ponies
Drag at their pickets.
The grass has gone brown in the summer —
(or is it the hay crop failing)

Pull an arrow out:
If you break it
The wound closes.
Salt is good too
And wood ashes.
Pounding it throbs in the night —
(or is it the gonorrhea)

CAPTIVES

Some came in chains
Unrepentant but tired.
Too tired but to stumble.
Thinking and hating were finished
Thinking and fighting were finished
Retreating and hoping were finished.
Cures thus a long campaign,
Making death easy

CHAMPS D'HONNEUR

Soldiers never do die well;
Crosses mark the places —
Wooden crosses where they fell,
Stuck above their faces.
Soldiers pitch and cough and twitch —
All the world roars red and black;
Soldiers smother in a ditch,
Choking through the whole attack.

RIPARTO D'ASSALTO

Drummed their boots on the camion floor,
Hob-nailed boots on the camion floor.
Sergeants stiff,
Corporals sore.
Lieutenant thought of a Mestre whore —
Warm and soft and sleepy whore,
Cozy, warm and lovely whore;
Damned cold, bitter, rotten ride,
Winding road up the Grappa side.
Arditi on benches stiff and cold,
Pride of their country stiff and cold,
Bristly faces, dirty hides —
Infantry marches, Arditi rides.
Grey, cold, bitter, sullen ride —
To splintered pines on the Grappa side
At Asalone, where the truck-load died.

MONTPARNASSE

There are never any suicides in the quarter among people one knows

No successful suicides.

A Chinese boy kills himself and is dead.

(They continue to place his mail in the letter rack at the Dome)

A Norwegian boy kills himself and is dead.

(No one knows where the other Norwegian boy has gone)

They find a model dead

Alone in bed and very dead.

(It made almost unbearable trouble for the concierge)

Sweet oil, the white of eggs, mustard and water soapsuds and stomach pumps rescue the people one knows.

Every afternoon the people one knows can be found at the cafe.

OILY WEATHER

The sea desires deep hulls —
It swells and rolls.
The screw churns a throb —
Driving, throbbing, progressing.
The sea rolls with love
Surging, caressing,
Undulating its great loving belly.
The sea is big and old —
Throbbing ships scorn it.

T. ROOSEVELT

Workingmen believed
He busted trusts,
And put his picture in their windows.
"What he'd have done in France!"
They said.
Perhaps he would —
He could have died
Perhaps,
Though generals rarely die except in bed,
As he did finally.
And all the legends that he started in his life
Live on and prosper,
Unhampered now by his existence.

ALONG WITH YOUTH

A porcupine skin
Stiff with bad tanning,
It must have ended somewhere.
Stuffed horned owl
Pompous
Yellow eyed;
Chuck-wills-widow on a biassed twig
Sooted with dust.
Piles of old magazines,
Drawers of boys letters
And the line of love
They must have ended somewhere.
Yesterdays tribute is gone
Along with youth
And the canoe that went to pieces on the beach
The year of the big storm
When the hotel burned down
At Seney, Michigan.

CHAPTER HEADING

For we have thought the larger thoughts
 And gone the shorter way.
And we have danced to devil's tunes,
 Shivering home to pray;
To serve one master in the night,
 Another in the day.

VALENTINE

For a Mr. Lee Wilson Dodd and Any of His Friends
Who Want It.

Sing a song of critics
pockets full of lye
four and twenty critics
hope that you will die
hope that you will peter out
hope that you will fail
so they can be the first one
be the first to hail
any happy weakening or sign of quick decay.
(All very much alike, weariness too great,
sordid small catastrophes, stack the cards on fate,
very vulgar people, annals of the callous,
dope fiends, soldiers, prostitutes,
men without a gallus*)
If you do not like them lads
One thing you can do
Stick them up your —— lads
My Valentine to you.

* . . . .